WRITTEN BLUES

IT TAKES INSANITY TO LOVE A MESS.

ANIRUDDH B.

Made with ♥ on the Notion Press Platform
www.notionpress.com

To everyone, I have ever loved and to everyone, I will ever love.

Contents

Preface

For the most part, this book has come from imagination and personal experiences. Most of those experiences have led to a pursuit of wonder about life and people. Taking into consideration that I previewed the same scenario with varied perspectives. An echo to a scream. Individuals over crowds. Although, this book is intended for everyone to read and explore, I certainly hope it is not shunned by others since, my effort is to gently remind that we all think these things; and walk through life not reciting what we actually mean. I hope you find a piece of yourself somewhere in these lines.

1. Merak

Up above the silent hill,
We were standing at out will.
When the flowers went black and the night grew dark,
There were no trace of sparks.
We felt insidious inside our hearts,
but the trouble won't forever last.
Whilst the midnight moon gazed upon the stars,
We knew a few things about each other's past.
At the break of dawn we tried to sleep,
Because your heels were too rough for the hills...
We were afraid to bow and lie,
But we laid down to watch the sky.

2. Mistaken for Strangers

8 minutes of darkness,
Silence of the seas,
The palm, the wind, the deep,
And this summer breeze.
8 minutes of darkness,
An avalanche of emotions,
Blizzarding through the still,
Deafening in their motion.
8 minutes of darkness,
And the living colours of my being,
Ruminating across the silent floor of the seas.
8 minutes of darkness,
And now the story begins,
Of our scintillating affair...
Down below the depths of this love so rare.

3. Interstellar

Table of a budding writer,
A page, a pen
A book of emotion.
Scars of the scarlet,
A mug, some dust
A reckless endeavor to cheat lust.
Spotless keys,
A pick, a clip
A pair of tired wrists,
with fingers spread adrift.
In this moment,
with my quivering heart,
I only write to fulfill what I start.
For my faith becomes destiny and
The story falls apart.

4. Q.U.A.R.A.N.T.I.N.E.D.

Bike rides and love bites,
Not just a man with insight.
Showcase your soul and find me whole
To nurture to shower,
All that I behold;
Comes back right to you,
I think I'll forever wait in that cue,
Time is an illusion, true...
I have deciphered the clues,
That you never sent through.
I guess I'm obsessed with being your man?
So many words for the broken heart,
Nothing left to see in this crimson love.
Rusted and edgy,
I fight for my serenity.
Fixing your flaws was not only my duty,
I took it as an emblem to carry.
Feminine and agile,
You belong with the Nile.
Can I mend your heart and make you fly?
Like blossoms of the eve dancing in the sky.
I'll take the liberty of being your messenger...
Cause in your perfection,
I found my answer.

5. Expressions

I'm not awake,
I'm wide asleep.
Got a gun in one and
A rose in my sleeve.
This ecstasy of us burning in love,
Has led me to decisions I can't un-turn.
Violence from words,
My heart somewhere hurts.
Craving for your trust,
I'm submerged.
Break this curse and lift me up…
I thought you were divine,
You're not even fairy dust.
Compensating for wealth,
Arguing in a shell.
I never asked to touch you but,
You know me so well.
Not by definition, but,
I declare this hell.
Want to love you so much more,
Got nothing left in my store.
It was easy building this up,
Watching it all go to dust,
In a single, unfamiliar hug.

6. Armageddon

Lost in space,
Travelling beyond destination.
Can't be your alibi,
I don't have a solution.
I was built to destroy,
You were the blossom .
I have not ever felt,
The connotion of Autumn.
Millions of miles away,
I can't hear your name.
Is it too far out for us to stay?
Let there be a way.
I have never missed,
But you are missing from me;
I pity the empty space.
Is this another story?
If there were no ink…
I'd have no pen,
I feel like a hyphen without prefix.
You're neither the summit I want conquered,
Nor the piece of puzzle I could bother.
Love comes in various ways,
This one was just torture.

7. Juvenile

You adapted me,
became me,
knew me thoroughly.
Because I was the only one who was there.
When you kept pushing everyone,
I was still there.
...and now
I am in your position;
I do not want to become you,
because you're all I have...
I want to pick you from a crowd.
I want to know that I am certain.
For once, in my life,
I do not want to fail at love.

8. Vanquish

You're the only peace in my life,
The reason why I survive.
They ain't lying when they tying,
Bounds we keep denying.
Denying the fact that our art is soul.
Inconspicuous, they never know
Delusions I understand
but, the context that follows.
Be free and confident with your writing,
People don't want to stop fighting.
The struggle is real,
And real is the brawl.
Can you no longer be Autumn?
I can't take the fall.

9. Theatrics

I asked you to stay,
I asked you sway.
You gave in to your fears,
To save a few tears.
The symphony of liers,
The truth that inspires,
Along the path of the blade,
Lacking what you made.
Testing what you break,
Hoping to find a cure,
A true emotion to play;
The vulgarity in May.

10. Pyro

Losing myself in you was madness,
Not torture although, at the brink.
Conjuring the capacity of weak,
The strength comes from within.
Falsifying the evidence and
Criminalising the source.
Coded words, empty roads,
Scintillating, the life down below.
Show me your colours,
Don't want your soul.
I am a wanderer on this rock,
Wishing not to grow old.

11. Axiom

In the end,
Our stories will fade.
With echoes of our kisses,
Flitting in the universe.
Ensuing the fragments of stardust,
Individual particles,
Hovering through the void.
Our letters to kin,
We tried to avoid.
The noise in this vaccum,
Stored in an android.
Whistling past the Andromeda,
Disoriented in it's wake,
The journey to stray.

12. Revelry

Winters remind me of you,
Still feeling the blues,
I no longer hope for a better hue,
At peace, within, is what you do.
Walking under the shadow of the moon,
Hold my hand, make this true.
I got nothing to envy,
I got all the jewels.
Further into the night,
Feeling the extent of sight.
Under the blanket, we fight,
Till our souls ignite.

13. Mayday

As I stand, beneath this tree,
The life I've lived, the dreams I see.
Elements, etymology and ecstacy,
Are all a cause of a certain mystery.
The myriad of words and
Oblivion in the skies,
Led me to this fight,
To conquer all that spites.
Fairly obvious, for the clandestine,
Nothing more that the clock could wind.
Only cause the toughest storms I've witnessed in life,
Had nothing to do with the weather outside.

14. Saturation

You want me to reminiscent,
To stay,
In order for our love,
To burn this way.
But I am too much fire,
I am too much flame.
To be in control of your thoughts,
Is a waste of my game.
The next time you see me,
I'll be tame,
So that you know,
You can't hold this mane.

15. Insieme

I reached within,
Asked her to be a part of my skin
I touched her silhouette with my fingertips,
Ensured that my brain does not drift.
Over the board as we went,
I noticed her soft tan hands.
I did not choke, I do not repent.
As we mellowed into the sin,
Not a trace of you within.
Were you hoping I would hurt?
Darling, what we had was never love.

16. Gang of Two

The words of her heart,
Are opaque in her eyes,
The pages of her book,
Are half open, half scorched like mine.
Piece by piece she melts away the pain,
The pages she couldn't find, no one to blame.
Didn't like her flow, no,
She did not like the flame.
But the fire was hers like the stars within.
Ash to ashes, word to words
Fickle smile through a glance,
The only story above.
Mirroring reflections, broken frames,
Fragments of reality, scintillating names.
Tired of the reasons, tired of the game.
Sustenance, morality and law,
Aren't they all the same?

17. Blaze

I am the kind of tired that sleep won't fix,
Drained and dead, the spark in the context.
Falling back to delusion,
Holding on too tight.
The storm was calm that night,
Rowing the boat,
Flowing the flow.
Pretty eyes is where I bow,
And the storm comes in,
Hold that thought.

18. Kalon

There's no answer to a rhetorical question,
But if you say yes, here's my conclusion
An aftermath of the emotions felt,
I'm the wind that controls your breath.
Hiding in plain sight,
As brilliant as the night sky.
Residing between those eyes,
The chemical that drains our rights.
Maybe a rhyme, maybe a crime,
There ain't much left for me to define.
What these words possess or
What is it that we digress?
There are no questions unanswered but,
Illusions we don't yet comprehend.

19. Comet

I'm not saying, I'm not saying
That I'd love you
In the cabin I built inside the woods.
I'm not saying, I'm not saying,
That I'd drift away.
Under the starlight we gazed.
I'm not saying, I'm not saying,
That the boat we sailed,
Has left our sight.
I'm not saying,
That the flowers won't blossom
If you left my side.
All I'm saying is,
You'd be wind to my sail
and the blood in my veins.
All I'm saying is,
My daze would be better,
If I lay with you at night.

20. Marvel

Existing in time,
Belonging to eternity.
Let me fill out the mess,
Take me to serenity.
Vibe higher,
Tune in to a different galaxy.
I wonder what energies can do,
When there's nothing left due.
Miles to go from where I sit,
Uncertainty at brisk.
Clinging on to faith,
Making the way as it is.

21. Chaos

Drown me in confessions,
Rejuvenate me in silence.
Let the world go out vibrant,
You should not go violent.
To occupy your space,
You got to put some weight,
Over on your shoulders
And let them weigh.
Down the road that says life,
Pass me the ink that survives.
Into the beyond, we go,
Forging our destiny as we know.
Mortgaging our souls,
Which could not be sold.
The paranoid won't bark
and the bark won't fruit.
Silent prayers of the will inside,
Trouble as it comes,
Will not leave without a fight.

22. Quantum

Because when I walked,
It was your hair I saw swinging,
In the cold, hollow wind,
Tragedy shot our wings.
With nothing left to avenge,
We did not vow for revenge,
When you passed by me,
I saw your reflection behind the rising.
The sun looked beautiful behind you,
In your shadow, I found my clue.
It was not your beauty that strikes,
But you entice insights.
Curling up words as you speak,
Hard rock playing in the jeep.

23. Solitude

I wish I enacted the way I thought,
Spontaneous and vivid.
With a quench for seas,
I'd have gulped the mountain breeze.
I'd push myself to oblivion.
Raw and unshaken like
a volcano in it's destruction.
Perhaps for them to know,
I only wear a gentle coat.

24. Echo

She was a stranger,
someone out of this universe.
Who immensly knew,
and willingly participated,
in the destruction of life
to awake humanity.

25. 1.9.7.3

I want a prized possesion,
like a shack by the sea.
Where there would be no one,
but you and me.
I want a prized possession,
like someone who'd care,
near someone who not just speaks,
but actually shares.
I want a prized possession,
like having the luck to see,
sunset besides the ocean everyday,
and that girl with me.

9 798889 758068

Printed by Libri Plureos GmbH in Hamburg, Germany